NEHRU AND THE TRIBALS

About the Author

Dr. S.S. Shashi (*b.* 1936), an eminent scholar and writer of over 95 books, holds Ph.D degree in Sociology and D.Litt. in Anthropology from abroad. The first Indian scholar to obtain D.Litt. in Anthropology on Roma, the Indian gypsies in the world. Subjects covered: social sciences, gypsology, nomadic studies, defence, poetry, travelogues, and children's literature. Received several awards from Central and the State Governments. Widely travelled in India and abroad. Anthropological works: *Nomads of the Himalayas, A Sociological Study of Gaddi Tribe of Himachal Pradesh, Tribal Women of India, Shepherds of India, Nightlife of Indian Tribes, Tribes of Himachal Pradesh, Our Tribal Children, Encyclopaedia of World Women, Roma: The Gypsy World and others.*

He is the Media Head in the Ministry of Information and Broadcasting, Government of India, New Delhi.

NEHRU AND THE TRIBALS

S.S. Shashi

CONCEPT PUBLISHING COMPANY PVT. LTD.
NEW DELHI-110059

ISBN: 978-81-7022-254-5

Edition 2026

Published and Printed by

Concept
Since 1974

Concept Publishing Company Pvt. Ltd.
A/15-16, Commercial Block, Mohan Garden,
New Delhi-110059 (India)
T: 91-11-41101460
E: publishing@conceptpub.com, *W*: www.conceptpub.com

DEDICATED
TO THE MEMORY
OF PANDITJI

The intoxicating fragrance
Of roses, to this day-
Since,
The twenty-seventh May
Of Sixty-Four-
Has nowhere been found,
In any garden
On the face of the earth.
Where has it gone then?
Questions kept on
Giving rise to more questions.
At long last,
A dry and withered petal
Of a rose, spoke out:
"There, where the gardener
Has gone!
There, where Nehru
Has gone!"

– Dr. S.S. Shashi

Rendering from a
Hindi poem by Bharati

Contents

List of Illustrations

Preface

JAWAHARLAL NEHRU was a man of the masses. He was the architect of the modern India who dedicated his whole life to the nation.

Panditji had many-faceted personality. He was a distinguished statesman, an able administrator, an eminent author and a great charmer. His charm was the result of his genuine love for his people and the country. He worked for the weak and the down-trodden. His humane concern for the tribal people and their development was remarkable. In this book I have tried to analyse the contribution of Jawaharlal Nehru to tribal development.

I studied the Indian tribes, in general, and the nomads of the Himalayas, in particular, for my doctorate and post-doctorate degrees. Besides, they had been subjects of numerous books and research articles, I have written. During such studies, I came across a treasure of literature that encompasses Nehru's love for tribals. Hence this book.

I have collected the material from various reports appeared in *'Vanyajati'* and Nehru's own writings and speeches that appeared from time to time.

I am grateful to the publishers and the writers whose writings had enriched this study.

S.S. SHASHI

THE WELL WISHER OF THE TRIBALS

Nehru and The Tribals

WHEN we remember the dynamic personality of Jawaharlal Nehru and his varied interests in different subjects, we recall his own words because we cannot put them better. He said: "If any people chose to think of me then I should like them to say–this was the man who with all his mind and heart loved India and the Indian people. And they in turn were indulgent to him and gave him their love most abundantly and extravagantly." These words depict how Nehru loved his people and how he got abundant love from them.

His humanitarian thinking, indomitable courage, wisdom, administrative ability, statesmanship and, above all, the charm of his magnetic personality have had a deep impact on our social, political and economic structures which he shaped in its formative years. He had unparalleled sincerity towards the people in general and weaker sections in particular. Though he had reached the Himalayan heights in every sphere of life, Panditji was the commonest among the commons and was always approachable to the common man.

FRIEND OF TRIBALS

Nehru was a great friend of tribals, and an ardent lover of their art and culture. His interest in the tribal people transcended the political, cultural and economic affinities of the tribals with the rest of the community. He regarded them as the repositories of original human culture of India. Their way of life to a great extent was still not adulterated by the complexities of the modern culture and civilization.

Nehru extended his sympathy to tribal people. Every year, he would spare some time from busy schedule to be with tribal folks coming from the distant tribal belts for the Republic Day celebrations in Delhi. He would sing and dance with them and forget for a moment the cares of a Prime Minister. Panditji was very critical about the vices that were replacing the virtues of the tribal social life in the name of civilization. He found the folk songs and dances more inspiring than the cinema and theatre. To him the open hostility of the tribal society seemed much better than the evil practices prevailing in the urban society.

He once said: "They are a virile people. I approach this simple folk in a spirit of comradeship and not like someone aloof who had come to look at them, examine them, weigh them or try and make them conform to another way of life".

BARRIER SHOULD GO

Nehru was even opposed to the terms of Scheduled Castes and Scheduled Tribes. He was proud to call himsèlf a tribal or a nomad and, therefore, wanted the barrier of separating Scheduled Castes and Scheduled Tribes should go.

He opposed the idea of keeping tribals as a separate class or group. Nehru had great admiration for tribal way of life. He liked their innocent behaviour, clean heart and straightforwardness. He once remarked: "They are an extremely disciplined people, often much more democratic than most others in India. Without a constitution and the rest, they function democratically and carry out the decisions made by their elders or their own representatives almost without exception. Above all, they are a people who sing and dance and try to enjoy life; not people who sit in stock exchanges and shout at each other and call that civilization. I would prefer any day to be a nomad in the hills to being a member of stock exchanges or being made to sit there and listen to those frightfully ugly noises. Is that the civilization we want the tribal people to have? I hope not. I am quite sure that ultimately the civilization of the tribal folk, of song and dance, will last when stock exchanges have ceased to exist in this country and other countries"

LOVER OF NATURE

Nehru had a poetic heart and was ardent lover of nature. He liked hills, rivers, trees and natural environment for which he desired to be a nomad and live among nomadic communities. It was Nehru, who helped the nomadic people, particularly Gadia Lohar of Rajasthan and

Gujjars of Kashmir and Himachal Pradesh, in rehabilitation. But this adjustment was not based on damaging the tribal or nomadic culture. His approach was different from theoretical anthropologists'.

I had the opportunity to work among nomads of the Himalayas, particularly Gaddis and Gujjars of Himachal Pradesh. Both the communities are nomadic and semi-nomadic.

Gujjars are mostly pastoral but Gaddis are semi-pastoral and a semi-agricultural tribe. They are simply, beautiful, fierce stalwart and virtuous race and are accustomed to enduring great hardships. They reside exclusively on the snowy ranges of Dholadhar which divide Chamba from Kangra in Himachal Pradesh. In my social anthropological survey of 300 families, on asking their views whether they still wanted to lead a nomadic life, a nomad said in an angry voice: "We are no more keen to lead the migratory life. Nobody likes to leave his home and hearth and wander hither and thither like nomads for six months of the year, except for the sake of belly."

The same sort of response I got from Gujjars also. Hence I concluded that the causes of nomadism among Gujjars and other Himalayan nomads in general and the Gaddis in particular are as under :

1. Scarcity of fodder for the flocks during the winter season.
2. Unsuitability of snowfall to the sheep and goats.
3. Scarcity of food stuffs as the yield of the crops is not up to the mark.
4. Non-availability of seasonal employment in the region.
5. Cultivation of land by a few in district Kangra for which they have to move.
6. Health-hazard of severe winter.
7. An urge to migrate because of a long-standing habit; and
8. Association of migration with the mythical migration of Lord Shiva from Kailash to Chamba during winter.

Only eight per cent responses, in our public opinion polls, were associated with certain conditions regarding their will to lead the migratory life; the remaining 92 per cent respondents felt the migration to be inconvenient. This data is different from what we got from Gadia

Lohars who roam from place to place in the plains and do not want to settle.

I have interviewed a large number of Gaddis, Gujjars and other nomads of the Himalayas from time to time while working in Ashok Ashram, Kalsi, Dehra Dun, with Pt. Dharm Dev Shastri. I had the privilege of attending the Gujjar nomadics' tribal conference addressed by Pt. Jawaharlal Nehru held at Choharpur in Dehra Dun district.

It will be interesting to note that Nehru was keenly interested in the rehabilitation of Gadia Lohars. A report appeared on Gadia Lohars in the context of Nehru's plan on rehabilitation says: Of all the great social workers, who took up the cause of these nomads to their heart, the person, whose contribution stands unique, is Shri Manikyalal Verma of Mewar. To him goes the credit of drawing the attention of the late Pandit Jawaharlal Nehru, the Prime Minister of India, towards the miserable plight of a section of teeming millions, who are termed as "Nomads" and popularly known as Gadia Lohars. Mr. Verma persuaded Pt. Nehru to take the lead in rehabilitating these people, who, as a patriotic gesture, voluntarily took to this wandering life, after the tragic fall of Chittorgarh, the capital of Sisodia Kings of Mewar, as a sequence of the siege laid by Mughal Emperor Akbar. Along with their Chief, Maharana Pratap Singh, the gallant and indomitable warrior lord of Mewar, who refused to yield though vanquished, these brave people also, all belonging to the warrior race, took a solemn pledge neither to live under a roofed house and lead a settled life, nor to enter Chittorgarh until that fort and their much beloved motherland was freed from the clutches of the victor.

True to this pledge, these people, as a class, kept on moving from one place to another all these 400 years, depending for their daily bread upon the sweat of their brow and the skill of their hands They are expert blacksmiths and, as such, fabricate and sell in the open market the iron implements necessary for every day use, for agricultural or domestic purposes. They travel in bullock-carts, which is their mobile home, housing the whole family of six or seven persons and their entire belongings, which they can claim as their own, under the sky. The unflinching faith in the vow their ancestors took and the resoluteness and intrepidity, with which they adhered to it all these years, have stood the test of time, and is unparalleled in the history of mankind.

Greatly touched by the heroic and patriotic gesture of this honest tribe, Pandit Jawaharlal Nehru readily gave his consent to lead the entry-procession of this patriotic race into the historic fort of Chittor. The bar that had prevented them so far from entering Chittor had been removed as their mother-land was freed from foreign subjugation. Their pledge was honoured as soon as India was declared "A Complete Sovereign State" in 1947; and now there was no hitch in giving up the nomadic career and leading a settled life. This great event took place in the year 1955.

It is claimed that nearly 400 families of these people got rehabilitated on that historic day.

I am told that those who settled down there sold their cattle and left the place again in search of jobs.

Nehru was also interested in Banjaras and Indian Roma Gypsies who left India over 1,500 years ago and still wandered from place to place in Europe and America. I had the opportunity to study these people indepth and found the educated Roma were aware that both Jawaharlal Nehru and Indira Gandhi had been very sympathetic to them. The groups of Roma Gypsies met Nehruji and Indira Gandhi whenever they came to India.

In his speech in Hindi, in Nomads' tribal conference in Dehra Dun, Nehru said "A few years ago I went to Chamba and Dalhousie and met Gujjars. I tried to understand their problems. This time Pt. Dharm Dev Shastri invited me to meet all of you. I believe, there should be equal opportunities for all in development. My heart likes to adopt nomadism and if I could get an opportunity, I would never sit at one place. Our country is very vast and I too wander here and there in the country and abroad. But the nomadism, which you have adopted, is no good. I don't say that you should not move but if you travel or wander only for your livelihood, it is an obstacle in your progress. In this conference we are discussing the handicaps in the way of progress. Gujjar Tribal Welfare Committee should work for your welfare. Gujjars of J&K, Punjab and Himachal Pradesh should associate with this organisation and exchange their views on problems. I like Gujjars. They are helping the nation by way of producing milk and ghee. I want the Gujjars should progress in all respects."

APPROACH TO TRIBAL PROBLEMS

Nehru as Prime Minister was directly concerned with the tribal policy and decision-making about the tribal problems. In his speeches and writings he always laid stress that the approach to the tribal people should be one of learning from them and, having learnt, of trying to help and co-operate with them.

In his foreword to the second edition of Verrier Elwin's *Philosophy for NEFA,* Nehru said: "It is between these two extreme positions that we have to function. Development in various ways there has to be, such as communications, medical facilities, education and better agriculture. These avenues of development should, however, be pursued within the broad framework of the following five fundamental principles:

1. People should develop along the lines of their own genius and we should avoid imposing anything on them. We should try to encourage in every way their own traditional arts and culture.

2. Tribal rights in land and forests should be respected.

3. We should try to train and build up a team of their own people to do the work of administration and development. Some technical personnel from outside will, no doubt, be needed, especially in the beginning. But we should avoid introducing too many outsiders into tribal territory.

4. We should not over-administer these areas or overwhelm them with a multiplicity of schemes. We should rather work through, and not in rivalry to, their own social and cultural institutions.

5. We should judge results not by statistics or the amount of money spent but by the quality of human character that is evolved."

Nehru was consistently opposed to any type of imposition on the tribals. He made it clear that we should help them to develop along the lines of their own tradition and genius. . . . Speaking on tribals' integration with national life, he said: "If you approach the tribal people with affection, go to them as a liberating force and as a friend so that they may feel you have come not to take away something from them but to give them something, that is the right integration. But if they feel you have come to change their methods of living, then it is all completely wrong".

WARNING

Nehru seriously considered the various tribal problems and warned the anthropologists, social workers and administrators not to adopt any extreme method to mend or deviate them from their pious and peaceful life.

In a foreword to the book entitled *A Philosophy for NEFA*, Nehru said: "We cannot allow matters to drift in the tribal areas or just not take interest in them. In the world of today that is not possible or desirable. At the same time we should avoid over-administering these areas and, in particular, sending too many outsiders into tribal territory"

TRIBAL LANGUAGE

Nehru was in favour of developing the tribal culture and oral literature through their own languages. He considered this problem exceedingly important from the psychological point of view. He announced that the Government would encourage the tribal languages. In this matter he was also influenced by Lenin and other leaders who won the goodwill of the tribal people of the Soviet Republic by encouraging hundreds of their dialects by preparing dictionaries and vocabularies and even by evolving new scripts.

There is rich oral literature in many tribal dialects, but there is not much literature available in their languages except Santhali or Oraon.

Nehru instructed that the people working in tribal areas should understand their languages – the man or woman whose mind and even more so whose heart understands the problems; who is an enthusiast in this cause, who does not go there just to sit in an office for a few hours a day and for the rest curse his luck at being sent to an out of the way place. Although he gave top priority to development of communica tions, schools, roads, etc., in the tribal areas, he made it clear that there should be no attempt to impose others' ways of life on them in a hurry. Let change come gradually and be worked out by the tribals themselves. In the light of these thoughts, he could understand the core and crux of the tribal problems in India.

Nehru was interested in everything that contributed towards the welfare of his country men. He understood the spirit of India, its strength and weaknesses and loved his people as they were. So also he had special love for tribal people which was mingled with respect for their culture and tradition. This special feeling of Nehru is reflected in his words and deeds which serve as beacon lights for generations to come.

SPEECHES ON TRIBALS

The author has collected the speeches of Panditji – related to tribals – delivered in Parliament, Tribal Conferences and other occasions. The same are reproduced in the next pages.

NEHRU ADDRESSING THE AUDIENCE

Speeches and Writings

THE TRIBAL PEOPLE*

MR. CHAIRMAN and friends, this audience is more or less a select one since it consists largely of experts. I am not an expert and I am afraid I shall not be able to contribute much if we were to sit down and discuss your problems.

I suppose you have invited me here because I happen to occupy the office of Prime Minister, but I think I have another, and possibly greater, claim to participate in this Conference. The claim is that I have always – long before I became Prime Minister – felt very strongly attracted to the tribal people of this country. This feeling was not the curiosity an idle observer has for strange customs; nor was it the attraction of the charitably disposed who want to do good to other people. I was attracted to them simply because I felt happy and at home with them. I liked them without any desire to do them good or to have good done to me. To do good to others is, I think, a very laudable desire but it often leads to great excesses which do not result in good to either the doer or the recipient.

In the tribal people I have found many qualities which I miss in the people of the plains, cities and other parts of India. It was these very qualities that attracted me.

The tribal people of India are a virile people who naturally went astray sometimes. They quarrelled and occasionally cut off each other's heads. These were deplorable occurrences and should have been checked. Even so, it struck me that some of their practices were

* Speech delivered at the opening session of the Scheduled Tribes and Scheduled Areas Conference held in New Delhi on June 7, 1952.

perhaps less evil than those that prevail in our cities. It is often better to cut off a hand or a head than to crush and trample on a heart. Perhaps I also felt happy with these simple folk, because the nomad in me found congenial soil in their company. I approached them in a spirit of comradeship and not like someone aloof who had come to look at them, examine them, weigh them, measure them and report about them or to try and make them conform to another way of life

I am alarmed when I see – not only in this country but in other great countries, too – how anxious people are to shape others according to their own image or likeness, and to impose on them their particular way of living. We are welcome to our way of living but why impose it on others? This applies equally to national and international fields. In fact, there would be more peace in the world if people were to desist from imposing their way of living on other people and countries.

I am not at all sure which is a better way of living. In some respects I am quite certain theirs is better. Therefore, it is grossly presumptuous on our part to approach them with an air of superiority or to tell them what to do or what not to do. There is no point in trying to make of them a second rate copy of ourselv..

Now, who are these tribal folk? A way of describing them is that they are the people of the frontiers or those who live away from the interior of this country. Just as the hills breed a somewhat different type of people from those who inhabit the plains, so also the frontier breeds a different type of people from those who live away from the frontier. My own predilection is for the mountains rather than for the plains, for the hill folk rather than the plains people. So also I prefer the frontier, not only in a physical sense but because the idea of living near a frontier appeals to me intellectually. I feel that it would prevent me from becoming complacent, and complacency is a very grave danger, especially in a great country like India, where the nearest frontier may be a thousand miles away.

We should have a receptive attitude to the tribal people. There is a great deal we can learn from them, particularly in the frontier areas, and, having learnt, we must try to help and co-operate. They are an extremely disciplined people, often a great deal more democratic than most others in India. Even though they have no constitution, they are able to function democratically and carry out the decisions made by elders or representatives. Above all, they are a people who sing and dance and try to enjoy life; not people who sit in stock exchanges, shout at each other and think themselves civilized.

I would prefer being a nomad in the hills to being a member of the stock exchange, where one is made to sit and listen to noises that are ugly to a degree. Is that the civilization we want the tribal people to have? I hope not. I am quite sure that the tribal folk, with their civilization of song and dance, will last until long after stock exchanges have ceased to exist.

It is a very great pity that we in the cities have drifted so far away from the aesthetic side of life. We still have a good many folk-songs and dances when we go to the villages, because modern civilization has more or less left them untouched. The progress of modern civilization in India involves both good things and bad. One of the things we have lost is the spirit of song and dance and the capacity for enjoyment and this is what the tribal people so abundantly have. We seem to pay too much attention to the cinema: it is undoubtedly an excellent medium for many good things, but unfortunately it has not proved to be particularly inspiring. We must imbibe something of the spirit of the tribal folk instead of damping it with our long faces and black gowns.

For half a century or more, we have struggled for freedom and ultimately achieved it. That struggle, apart from anything else, was a great liberating force. It raised us above ourselves, it improved us and hid for the moment some of our weaknesses. We must remember that this experience of hundreds of millions of Indian people was not shared by the tribal folk. Our struggle for freedom did influence the tribes in Central India to some extent but the frontier areas of Assam, for instance, remained almost unaffected by it. This was partly due to the inadequacy of the means of communication available to us in the old days. Of course, there were other reasons too.

One of the reasons was that the city people were a little afraid to leave their familiar haunts and go into the mountains. The Christian missionaries went to various tribal areas and some of them spent practically all their lives there. I do not find many instances of people from the plains going to the tribal areas to settle down. Apart from our own lack of initiative, we were not allowed to go there by the British authorities, then in power. That is why our freedom movement reached these people only in the shape of occasional rumours. Sometimes they reacted rightly and sometimes wrongly, but that is beside the point.

The essence of our struggle for freedom was the unleashing of a liberating force in India. This force did not even affect the frontier people in one of the most important tribal areas. The result is that while we have had several decades in which to prepare ourselves psychologically for basic changes, the tribal people have had no such opportunity. On the contrary, they were prepared the other way round through the efforts of the British officials and sometimes the missionaries.

The missionaries did very good work there and I am all praise for them but, politically speaking, they did not particularly like the changes in India. In fact, just when a new political awareness dawned on India, there was a movement in North-Eastern India to encourage the people of the North-East to form separate and independent States. Many foreigners resident in the area supported this movement. I do not understand how it could be considered practical or feasible from any point of view. My point is that the people of the North-East frontier had been conditioned differently during the past generation and even in more recent years. The fault lay partly with us and partly with circumstances. These factors have an important bearing on any genuine understanding of the tribal folk

They are our own people and our work does not end with the opening of so many schools and so many dispensaries and hospitals. Of course, we want schools and hospitals and dispensaries and roads and all that but to stop there is rather a dead way of looking at things. What we ought to do is to develop a sense of oneness with these people, a sense of unity and understanding. That involves a psychological approach.

You may talk day after day about development programmes in regard to schools and other matters but you will fail completely if you do not touch the real core of the problem. The need, today, is to understand these people, make them understand us and thus create a bond of affection and understanding. After the achievement of independence, the basic problem of India, taken as a whole, is one of integration and consolidation. Political integration is now complete but that is not enough. We must bring about changes much more basic and intimate than mere political integration. That will take time, because it is not merely a matter of law. All we can do is to nurture it and create conditions where it finds congenial soil. So, the greatest problem of India today is, not so much political as psychological integration and consolidation. India must build up for herself a unity which will do away with provincialism, communalism, and the various other "isms" which disrupt and separate.

As I said, we must approach the tribal people with affection and friendliness and come to them as a liberating force. We must let them feel that we come to give and not to take something away from them. That is the kind of psychological integration India needs. If, on the other hand, they feel you have come to impose yourselves upon them or that we go to them in order to try and change their methods of living, to take away their land and to encourage our businessmen to exploit them, then the fault is ours, for it only means that our approach to the tribal people is wholly wrong. The less we hear of this type of integration and consolidation of the tribal areas, the better it will be.

We ought to be careful about appointing officers any where, but we must be doubly so when we appoint them in tribal areas. An officer in the tribal areas should not merely be a man who has passed an examination or gained experience of routine work. He must be a man with enthusiasm, whose mind and, even more so, whose heart understands the problem it is his duty to deal with. He must not go there just to sit in an office for a few hours a day and for the rest curse his fate at being sent to an out of the way place. That type of man is completely useless. It is far better to send a totally uneducated man who has passed no examination, so long as he goes to these people with friendship and affection and lives as one of them. Such a man will produce better results than the brilliant intellectual who has no human understanding of the problem. The man who goes there as an officer must be prepared to share his life with the tribal folk. He must be prepared to enter their huts, talk to them, eat and smoke with them, live their lives and not consider himself superior or apart. Then only can he gain confidence and respect, and, thus, be in a position to advise them.

The language problem is almost always exceedingly important from the psychological point of view. The best of solutions can come to nought if misunderstood or misinterpreted by the party concerned. It is absolutely clear to me that the Government must encourage the tribal languages. It is not enough simply to allow them to prevail. They must be given all possible support and the conditions, in which they can flourish, must be safeguarded. We must go out of our way to achieve this.

In the Soviet Republic we have the example of a country that has adopted such a policy with success. Lenin and other leaders in his time were exceedingly wise in this respect. Regardless of their ultimate objective, they wanted to win the goodwill of the people, and they won it largely by their policy of encouraging their languages, by going out of their way to help hundreds of dialects, by preparing dictionaries and vocabularies and sometimes even by evolving new scripts where there were none. They wanted their people to feel that they were free to live their own lives and they succeeded in producing that impression.

In the matter of languages there must be no compulsion whatsoever. I have no doubt at all that the West Bengal Government must have built special schools in places like Darjeeling and Kalimpong for the Tibetan-speaking people. If the tribal people have a script we must, of course, use it. But normally they do not have a script and the only script they have thus far learnt, to some extent, is the Roman script. It is a good script no doubt; and because many people have learnt it, I would not discourage it.

But if we are to evolve a script—here I do not speak with any assurance but am merely saying something that has occurred to me — it might be better, for the future, if we were to use the Devanagari script. It is a relatively easy script, apart from the fact that it can put the tribal folk more in touch with the rest of India than any other script. In areas where a majority of the people know the Roman script, I would not suddenly force them to abandon it because I do not want them to feel compelled in any way.

I find that so far we have approached the tribal people in one of two ways. One might be called the anthropological approach in which we treat them as museum specimens to be observed and written about.

To treat them as specimens for anthropological examination and analysis – except in the sense that everybody is more or less an anthropological specimen – is to insult them. We do not think of them as living human beings with whom it is possible to work and play. The other approach is one of ignoring the fact that they are something different requiring special treatment and of attempting forcibly to absorb them into the normal pattern of social life. The way of forcible assimilation or of assimilation through the operation of normal factors would be equally wrong.

In fact, I have no doubt that, if normal factors were allowed to operate, unscrupulous people from outside would take possession of tribal lands. They would take possession of the forests and interfere with the life of the tribal people. We must give them a measure of protection in their areas so that no outsider can take possession of their lands or forests or interfere with them in any way except with their consent and goodwill. The first priority in tribal areas, as well as elsewhere in the country, must be given to roads and communications. Without that, nothing we may do will be effective. Obviously, there is need for schools, for health relief, for cottage industries and so on. One must always remember, however, that we do not mean to interfere with their way of life but want to help them live it.

NEFA*

I visited parts of the hill areas of Assam, the North-East Frontier Agency, Manipur and Tripura.

These places are cut off from the rest of the World and can only be reached normally by long marches along the mountains. Supplies are sent to them by air and are dropped from the aircraft.

I do not know what ideas most people in India have about tribal folk. My own general impression has been largely derived from such people as the Bhils, the Santhals, the Gonds, etc. For my part I like these somewhat backward or even primitive people, but I recognize that they are primitive in their normal ways of life. Given the oppor-

* Speech delivered from tour of North-East Frontier Agency in 1952.

tunity, however, some of them can make good in other ways also. During my visit to the North-East Frontier, I had to change my conception of these tribes. I found a great variety of them, differing from each other very greatly. Some of them were undoubtedly rather primitive, but many of them were remarkably developed and advanced. Indeed, it is quite absurd to call them backward. An average crowd of some of these tribes would probably be more advanced in many ways than an average crowd elsewhere in India.

What appealed to me about all these tribal people was not only their physique and health and straight-limbed bodies but their frank demeanour. They looked one in the face and were not afraid or inhibited, men and women alive altogether they struck me as a fine lot of which any country can be proud. Almost everywhere there was a passion for education. The two principal demands were for roads and schools. I can well imagine that given these communications and schools, they would advance rapidly and be a credit to the country in many ways.

All these tribes and other people in these areas were almost completely cut off from the rest of India during British rule. Few of them came out of their areas and few from outside went there.

The first problem we have to face there is to inspire them with confidence and to make them feel at one with India, and to realise that they are part of India and have an honoured place in it. This can only be done by allowing them to retain their own cultural traits and habits and leaving them to develop along their own lines without any compulsion from outside.

The problem of these areas is to make the people feel that they have perfect freedom to live their own lives and to develop according to their wishes and genius. India to them should signify not only a protecting force but a liberating one. Any conception that India is ruling them and that they are the ruled, or that the customs and habits with which they are unfamiliar are going to be imposed upon them, will alienate them and make our frontier problems more difficult. I was glad to see that the Governor of Assam, Shri Jairamdas Doulatram, was very sympathetic and friendly to the tribal people and fully appreciated the policy that we had laid down. His chief difficulty, and indeed this is a common complaint, was lack of funds. Schools are relatively cheap and they are in a big demand. Communications are expensive, and, yet, without communications nothing can be done. During the British period these areas were left completely undeveloped and it is exceedingly difficult now to move about in the interior.

I would say that all this North-East border area deserves our special attention, not only of the Governments, but of the people of India. Our contacts with them will do us good and will do them good also. *They add to the strength, variety and cultural richness of India.* As one travels there, a new and vaster picture of India comes before the eyes and the narrowness of outlook, which sometimes obsesses us, begins to fade away. One feels that India is not just one particular part which we might know intimately, but something infinitely more, a meeting place of all manner of races, languages and cultures. Rabindranath Tagore wrote one of his famous poems about India:

> "No one knows at whose call so many streams of men flowed in restless tides from places unknown and were lost in one sea: here Aryan and non-Aryan, Dravidian, Chinese, the bands of Sakas and the Hunas and Pathan and Mogul, have become combined in one body"

In June, 1952, I addressed the conference of Scheduled Tribes and Scheduled Areas held in New Delhi. The speech I delivered at that time, though given on the spur of the moment, came to be looked upon as some kind of a statement of policy in regard to the tribal areas. Indeed it was printed and largely circulated in the North-Eastern areas, and quotations from it were often made in the addresses presented to me. This speech has thus assumed an importance which it was not originally meant to have. On reference being made to it in Assam and elsewhere, I went back to it myself and read it. I found that it did represent fairly clearly a certain approach to this problem of the tribes and that my new experience in North-East Frontier confirmed my previous views.

APPROACH*

I heard of this conference only three days ago when Mrs. Khongmen told me about it. It struck me immediately that it would be a great idea to have such a conference and I was surprised that it had been delayed so long, although I confess I do not particularly like to give trouble to various State Ministers to rush forward and backward between Delhi and their States. We, here in Delhi, have quite a number of Ministries, and conferences are arranged at the least provocation. They are so many that I think some check is necessary. This conference, however, is a good idea.

When we talk about tribal people, I wonder whether we all have the same idea in mind. So far as I am concerned, we are all tribals, whether we live in Delhi or Madras or Bombay or Calcutta or in the hills or in the plains. To call some people primitive and to think of ourselves as highly civilized is basically wrong. There are differences, of course. There are marked differences, for example, between the people of the Punjab and the people of Madras. There are differences between people living in the hills and people living in the plains. Geography and climate account for differences of food and clothing and living conditions. That is inevitable. We are very different, for example, from the Chinese or the Japanese, and yet, perhaps, there is something more in common between us and the Chinese and the Japanese than there might be between us and some people in Europe. On the other hand, there is something more in common between us and Europeans in language. All this proves that differences are of several kinds. But I am sure that to think of the tribals and non-tribals as people qualitatively different is wrong. Take the description in our Constitution of the Scheduled Castes. As you know, it is rather arbitrary. Government, after consideration, decides whether a particular caste is a Scheduled Caste or not. It is not possible to draw a hard and fast line. That is why we aim ultimately at removal of all these appellations, descriptions and names which ideologically and physically separate the people as the Depressed Classes, the Harijans, the Scheduled Castes, the Scheduled Tribes, and so on. Differences in customs and ways of living will con-

* Inaugural address at the Tribal Affairs Conference, New Delhi, December 4, 1954.

tinue to remain, because they are due to geography and climate. But this barrier of 'So and so belongs to a Scheduled Caste' should go.

There is at present a Backward Classes Commission sitting under the chairmanship of Kaka Kalelkar. Many of the Backward Classes are as backward as any of the Scheduled Castes. In fact, some are more backward. The essential problem, therefore, is to help all those who are backward. Let us recognize the fact that in India only a handful belong to the so-called superior class.

They are not necessarily different from the rest of the population but because, they have had greater opportunities of growth, education and better living conditions for generations and centuries they have assumed a relatively more important position in India. Inevitably, of course, some individuals go ahead of others. But it is not a good thing for castes and groups to be permanently installed in superior positions. Every individual should have openings and opportunities for advancement. The real problem thus is of raising the level of all depressed humanity in India, not this group or that group. We shall never succeed if we proceed group by group. That really brings us to the much wider problem of education and employment. We talk of basic education. We frequently adopt resolutions about it. The fact is that we have done very little about real basic education in the country.

All these general observations apply as much to tribals as to any other people. I want to stress that we must cease to think of our being different from the so-called tribal people. This vicious idea and superiority complex must go. Many of the tribal people have reached a high degree of development. In fact, I found that in some places the tribal people are better educated and disciplined and lead a better corporate life than the caste-ridden society that we suffer from.

We in India are being powerfully affected by all kinds of world economic problems in what may be called a market economy. To succeed in that economy one needs certain qualities. Normally speaking, these tribal areas have not come within the scope of a market economy which is governed by the rule of the survival of the fittest. It has, therefore, become necessary, as our Constitution has laid down, that we should prevent the incursion of the market economy into these people's areas. We shall have to prevent rich people from acquiring land and dispossessing the tribal people. We do not want the economy of the tribal areas to be upset. We want the tribal areas to advance in peace.

Looking at areas outside India which are inhabited by so-called primitive people, we find that two things affect them injuriously: introduction of a market economy during the last century or so, and next the introduction of gin and other alcoholic drinks from Europe. These two served to put an end to their traditional handicrafts and arts. They gave up their simple ways of living and adopted the so-called European civilization, which was most disastrous. To some extent, there is danger of the so-called Indian civilization having a similar disastrous effect, if we do not apply proper checks.

It is obvious that the tribal areas have to progress. Nobody wants to keep them as museum specimens. It is equally obvious that they have to progress in their own way. They do not like something alien to be imposed upon them. No individual can grow in alien surroundings, habits, or customs. How are we going to reconcile these two considerations? They are two extreme approaches. One is the museum approach, keeping them as interesting specimens for anthropologists to discuss. The other may be called the 'open door' approach. Both are equally bad. The second approach attracts all the undesirables from outside who exploit these people economically and otherwise and take them out of their moorings. We have to find a middle course. That can succeed only if there is no element of compulsion about it. That attempt has in fact to be made through their own people. The first thing, therefore, is to train their own people. That would be far more effective than for outsiders to work for them. We have to make them progress, but progress does not mean an attempt merely to duplicate what we have got in other parts of India. What is good in the rest of India will, of course, be adopted by them gradually. Imposition has to be absent as far as possible, and people have to be trained to train others. The progress may not be very rapid but we must remember that training takes time. Whatever profession you may adopt, engineering or medicine, it takes years to train people. It is better to go ahead on a systematic basis than by an 'odd job' approach.

JAGDALPUR CONFERENCE*

I have gone far and wide in our country Bharat. But this is the first time that I have come to Jagdalpur, in Bastar. I had a desire to visit this area as Adivasis live here. I had a keen desire to meet them and this has been fulfilled today. But I am sorry, I have come to stay here only for a short while. If I had more time, I would have gone to your villages, met you all and conversed with you all.

It was only two or three months ago – on our last Republic Day, i.e., 26th January, some of the villagers from your area had come to Delhi – the Capital of India, for giving a dance performance. They performed a very nice dance there. People from all over India had come there and you might be aware that the people from this place came in flying colours. I have seen today your folk dances, separately of different communities, and I have found them quite enchanting. I hope you will keep up this art of yours and will make more progress in it. I want that in our country, songs and dances should develop much and that people should do their work happily. You should not think that you have to leave your songs and dances. They are not bad.

Who constitutes these categories of Adivasis? I have not been able to solve this puzzle. In my opinion all of us are Adivasis – our Governor, Shuklaji and all of us. I do not like this distinction. We are all Adivasis. Yes, there may be some differences. In our country there are different kinds of castes, where several castes are prevalent, whether they call themselves Brahmins or Kshatriyas, they are all Adivasis. We have to abolish all distinctions of high and low. The place where you reside is a very beautiful one. Wherever you live, you should live in your own way. This is what I want. You have to decide yourselves how you would like to live. Your old customs and habits are good. We want that they should survive. But at the same time this distinction of hierarchy of castes has to be abolished and uprooted from our country. We want that you should be educated and should do your part in the welfare of our country. Our country is free now. We have achieved Swarajya. What does Swarajya mean? In our country there is no king

---

* Inaugural address at the Third Tribal Welfare Conference held at Jagdalpur, March 13, 1955.

or emperor. In our country we have our Rashtrapati (President). He is Dr. Rajendra Prasad. He had been to this place and must have met you. Who is our Rashtrapati? He is neither a king nor an emperor. He is like us. He had been a farmer from Bihar. Gone are the days of kings and emperors. Now the people of our country have to live in equality and to progress and be educated. How did our Rashtrapati come to this position? Because the people liked him, accepted him and elected him to be the Rashtrapati. Now, I am the Prime Minister of this country. How did I become the Prime Minister? Because the people elected me for the place. So, whomsoever the people elect, he rises to the highest position in the country. He will retain his position so long as the people want him to be there. Many people live in our country. There are many castes. Everyone of them has the right to become the Prime Minister or the Rashtrapati of the country. You too have got the same right. Any competent man from amongst you can become the Prime Minister or Rashtrapati of this country.

In this country there are many Gond brethren. I had some old friends among these Gond brethren. Sometimes I used to go to a village of the Gonds. I found them very healthy. I feel that if you get an opportunity to learn something more you can make much progress in your lives and your customs and traditions can also survive. You have to bear in mind that we all belong to our country Bharat. We are all equal and we have all equal shares and rights in our country and we have all to forge our country ahead. You had been to Delhi. You might have seen that people from far and wide come there. Delhi is our Capital. There is a lot of important work before us. The country has a large population. Their welfare and progress are to be achieved. All this work has to be done. Many big plans and projects have been framed for them. The question arises before us what is to be done for them? We generally speak of the Government. Who is this Government? I have already told you that no king or emperor remains now. There was British Government. They have also quitted our country. Now you are the Government. You are yourself the Government. There is no other Government. The people of India are the Government. The people who live in the villages are the real Government. But how is the management of this country to be carried on? How it should function? We have to devise some ways and means. For the administration of the country, one headman is elected. You yourself elect him – whether you elect Dr. Rajendra Prasad or any man from your province, district or tehsil. And this you have to do. You are the master – the people of this country are the masters and you know that the people elected by you form the Government.

You know that in your tribe also you have your rules and regulations and all of you strictly follow them. If you do not follow them, there will be some disorder. In the same way, there are laws and rules in the country. Laws and rules are codified. They are codified after consulting the views of the general public. Hence they are to be followed and obeyed by the public. Otherwise confusion and chaos would prevail. Whatever we have to do for our country, let us do it collectively. Let us do in consultation and with the co-operation of all; and then only we can prosper. You have to bear one thing in your mind that whether you reside here in Bastar or at Delhi or in any other part of the country we are all sailing in the same ship in the sea. You must remember that unless all of us propel the ship in a right manner, we are doomed to be drowned in water. Therefore, we all have to do our jobs in close co-operation and to forge ourselves and our country ahead to achieve progress and prosperity.

It is seven years since Swarajya dawned on our country. Many things have happened during these seven years. Our country has advanced far. But it is our desire that she should take more rapid strides and rapid progress be made. We have many big problems before us. We have all assembled here to devise ways and means of how we can serve Adivasis best and how they can prosper. We have to think and ponder over it. This is a big problem before us. The Adivasis of our country should learn, be educated and cultivate their lands and see that our country progresses. We want that your customs, traditions and religion should not be interfered with. Some people say that they should be changed. But I do not like it. I want that such arrangement should be made that you should decide for yourself how you would like it to be. Your own organization should remain, songs and dances should survive and at the same time you have to work for the progress and prosperity of the great country of ours, i.e., Bharat. We shall take your advice and co-operation in the administration of the country. You should once more remember that the Swarajya which you have achieved is not of your alone, but it is of all – of mothers, sisters, sons and daughters. This country is yours and none else can claim it. You have the same right to it as anyone else has. We all have to march ahead and to progress. We should not have an autocratic form of Government.

I got an opportunity to meet you all. When I happen to come next, I shall go to your villages and meet you all in person.

You see there is a big shield kept there which your dancing party brought from Delhi. They performed a very beautiful dance there. This is the reward of that performance. This is very nice thing. This shows what nice dances are performed by you.

Our country is Bharat. This country of ours, i.e., Bharat, has many names; Bharat Varsha, Bharat, Hindustan; in English we call her India and it is also called Hind. You might have heard that we often say 'Jai Hind' 'Bharat Mata Ki Jai'. What is the meaning of 'Bharat Mata Ki Jai'? It means 'Victory to the people of the country' in other words 'Victory to you'. Mother India is not a woman in flesh and blood. We ourselves are Mother India, you are Mother India. We are all small ingredients of the Mother India. To say 'Bharat Mata Ki Jai' means victory to the people of the country. So when I say Jai Hind, you also join with me and say Jai Hind thrice. Jai Hind! Jai Hind! Jai Hind!

RESOLUTIONS PASSED

Resolution No. 1: *Second Five-Year Plan–Framing of Tribal Welfare Schemes*

The Conference resolves that the Central and State Governments be requested that while framing the schemes for tribal welfare under the Second Five-Year Plan, they should take the advice and seek co-operation of tribal MLAs, tribal MPs and the non-official organizations working for the welfare of the tribals before finalizing them.

Resolution No. 2: *Second Five-Year Plan–Priority of Schemes*

The Conference is of opinion that while framing the schemes for tribal welfare, the foremost thing to be borne in mind is that the means for the physical development of the tribals and the necessary facilities thereof should be created so that the necessaries of life like pure water and healthy food, etc., are easily made available to them.

Resolution No. 3: *Economic, Social and Cultural Survey of Tribal Areas*

The Conference expresses its satisfaction that under the First Five-Year Plan, Community Development Projects and National Extension Service Blocks are being opened in large numbers in tribal areas. But at the same time it is of the opinion that unless a survey is taken of the physical, economic, social and cultural backgrounds of the tribal areas, it is not possible to assess the exact results and achievements of those projects. Therefore, this Conference requests the Central and the State Governments that arrangements should be made immediately to conduct a survey in the tribal areas. Before a complete survey is made, it is necessary that to start with, a sample survey of at least the important tribes of every State should be undertaken and completed within three years. In this work, necessary help should be sought from the Universities, Social Welfare Institutions and Bharat Sevak Samaj. The Central Government is requested to give financial help to the State Governments under Article 275 of the Constitution for the purpose of conducting this survey.

Resolution No. 4: *Local Contributions for Tribal Welfare Schemes*

The Conference is of opinion that for the implementation of the Community Development Projects, National Extension Service Blocks and other Development Schemes, the policy of fixing the proportion of local contributions as at present should be changed in accordance with the financial conditions of the tribals of the areas concerned. As the tribals are very backward, the practical aspects of the schemes should be settled according to the local conditions.

Resolution No. 5: *Trained Personnel for Tribal Welfare Work*

(a) The Conference is of the opinion that arrangements should be made immediately to give training to the non-official workers and Government officials working in the tribal areas and that a Committee should be formed for this purpose. Shri L.M. Shrikant, Vice-President of Bharatiya Adimjati Sevak Sangh, is empowered to nominate the members of the Committee. This Committee should submit its report within three months to the Executive Committee of the Sangh. The Committee should present its report on the period of training, its syllabus and other matters relating to it.

(b) Non-official tribal welfare workers and Govt. officials should be given training by competent and recognized institutions.

(c) The Conference requests the Commissioner for Scheduled Castes and Scheduled Tribes, Govt. of India, that for non-official institutions or State Governments getting grant from the Central Government, the training of non-official workers and Govt. officials should be made compulsory. A maximum time limit should also be fixed for it.

Resolution No. 6: *Medical Aid to Tribals*

In the tribal areas, medical help and facilities are almost negligible. Therefore, to encourage and attract medical men to serve in tribal areas, special allowances should be paid to them according to local conditions.

Wherever it is not possible to have a dispensary to give medical aid, mobile dispensaries should be started.

Resolution No. 7: *Primary Education up to Second Standard*

The Conference is of the opinion that in those Scheduled Areas where tribal dialects are prevalent, primary text-books in Nagari and provincial script should be prepared for the purpose of imparting education up to Second Standard to the tribal boys and girls in their own dialect. The Conference, therefore, requests the State Governments to take necessary steps in this direction.

THE NAGAS*

Mr. Deputy Speaker, Sir, I have welcomed this debate on the situation in the Naga Hills, not because it is grave from a military point of view,

* Speech in Lok Sabha, New Delhi, during debate on the Naga Hills situation, August 23, 1956.

but because it is essentially the kind of problem in which this House and Parliament should take interest.

Some Hon'ble Members have described it as a political problem and not a military problem. Well, if we had treated it as a military problem only, the results would probably have been very different. It is because we have not treated it as a purely military problem and have issued instructions, restrictions, limitations and inhibitions to our Army, that from the military point of view progress has not been as fast as it could have been. I believe that if we had treated it in a merely military way, we would not have won the goodwill and co-operation of the Nagas. I should like this House to remember that they should look at this in the larger context of our general policy in these areas, not only in the Naga Hills but in the North-East Frontier Agency (NEFA) and neighbouring areas. Many of these areas were for the first time brought under some kind of administration during the last six to eight years. This House will not probably find a parallel to the manner in which the administrative system spread out so peacefully and with such few incidents. That has been possible because we have issued strict injunctions and directions to the effect that we must win over the people and seek their co-operation. We have to build, whatever we do, on their goodwill.

There have been incidents, but very few. One major incident which the House might remember took place some three years ago. In Achaigmori, in the NEFA area, in October 1953 an officer of ours, with a number of troops, was going there, not to shoot or kill but on normal patrol and inspection work. They were suddenly and most unexpectedly attacked. The poor officer was taking a cup of tea in his camp, and the others were putting up tents. Seventy persons were killed-40 porters and 30 Army personnel. Seventy is a large number, and an occurrence of this kind naturally produces strong reactions in any government. But I doubt if any government in the world would have dealt with the situation the way we did. I must say that when we first heard of this incident, it made us and our Army rather angry. This was no battle, but sheer cold-blooded murder. However, we immediately recovered from the first shock and surprise and anger. Of course, we sent more force there, but we told them to bear in mind that it was no good killing the hostiles and burning their villages. An Hon'ble Member has reminded us that the normal thing in British times was to go and burn the villages, since bombing would not be effective in an area where people live in a scattered manner. But we would not do that. The place was very much in the interior and it took our forces a good deal of time and trouble to get there. Many months were needed to deal with the situation. We dealt with it essentially in a peaceful way. Ultimately we captured the people who were suspected of being guilty, and we handed them over to the tribal councils to judge.

I mention this incident of nearly three years ago to show how we approach these matters and how we issue instructions to the civilian officers and to our Army to deal with the situation in a peaceful way.

There was some trouble last year in the Tuensang area, which is largely a Naga area. It is all very well for the Hon'ble Members, Shri K.K. Basu and Shri H.V. Kamath, to say that we must deal with it in a human way and not send the Army. But then, what exactly is to be done when other people start killing? Do we send them messages of goodwill, or do we try to stop the killing? The population of that area sought our help. We received appeals from the villagers and from Government employees, teachers and others, asking for protection. Was it not our duty to give them protection? That is what happened in the Tuensang area. We had to send some of our forces with rifles and we did it without fuss. It was easy enough for us to treat the situation differently. But we proceeded slowly, because we had the object of winning them over and not merely crushing them. We had of course to shoot some because they shot at us. However, the Tuensang problem was solved within a few months without too much fuss.

When fighting was taking place in the Tuensang area, the Naga Hills were relatively quiet. There might have been some small incidents. At that time, Phizo had come to see the Governor and the Chief Minister of Assam. Actually, he issued statements more or less declaring his adherence to non-violence. But we found that while he said so and issued notices to that effect, he was actually preparing for violence. There is no doubt about it. He was inciting the people and telling them: "These statements about peaceful methods are a trick, just to give you greater chance to go ahead. Let us play this game here, and you carry on your activities there."

I want to give the Hon'ble Members some idea of who the Nagas are. The Nagas, correctly speaking are not what might be called a tribe or a single group of tribes closely tied to one another. I do not know when the word Naga came to be used. I have an idea that it is a British word, that is, that the word was used in the British times. I am not sure. But the tribes are named differently, Sema, Ao and Angami and so on. They do not call each other Nagas. This is a word which you and I may use and the British used. It was probably used in derision, because Naga means naked. But the biggest tribes are the Sema, Ao and Angami. If you go to this area, you will find that there is no common Naga language. The language or dialect changes every few miles, every half dozen villages.

Some tribes among the Nagas are what might be called the dominant tribes, militarily stronger or tougher than the others. The tribes which dominate the others receive some tribute from the other tribes. Some of these strong tribes, if they did not get tributes, have all along in the past taken strong action against the defaulting tribes.

Some figures about the Nagas might interest the Hon'ble Members. I am, of course, using the word Naga as a generic term. The population at present all over the areas – not the Naga area alone – is a little over half a million. In the Naga Hills District, the population is a little over two lakhs. In the Tuensang Frontier Division, also, the population is slightly over two lakhs. In the Tirap Frontier Division, it is 50,000 and in Manipur State, it is 80,000. The total is a little over 500,000, which is spread out over a large area. I confess that when I heard about Nagas as such about 25 years ago, I was rather attracted by what I had heard. Then came the case of that lady to whom reference was made by Shri Kamath – Rani Guidallo – who, after suffering a long period of imprisonment, was released some years ago. I am glad to say that proper arrangements were made for her to live in the house which she built for herself and for which we gave her help. We made as much reparation as we could for the misdeeds of the previous Government.

Shri Jaipal Singh referred to the deputation of people who came to see me. Shri Phizo and a number of his colleagues met me twice here. Shri Keishing has said something about an incident at Kohima, where, according to him, the Nagas came and were prevented from giving me an address, and, therefore, they became angry and walked away. The facts are somewhat different. I went to Kohima. The Prime Minister of Burma had also come over, flying across the frontier. He met me at Manipur, and we were going to Burma a day or two later. I thought I might utilize that opportunity to visit Kohima. We went to Kohima and we relaxed. I suggested to the authorities there that some kind of a welcome might be given to the Burmese Prime Minister. He was our guest and the people gathered to say a few words. It was not a normal visit of mine to that place. What I found later was that Nagas there wanted to read out an address to me. The Deputy Commissioner told them: " You can hand it over to the Prime Minister afterwards; I cannot allow your reading it out to him at a meeting when the Prime Minister of Burma and others have come". It is not, therefore, correct to say that I refused to take the address. As a matter of fact, on a previous occasion at Kohima I had actually met the Naga leaders (Shri Phizo was not there), discussed the matter with them and taken a long document from them. That was just a year earlier, and so it is not true to say that I refused to receive an address or that the Deputy Commissioner came in the way. But he did come in the way of an address being read at the meeting. I did not know it at that time; I knew it only later. Then, when U Nu and I arrived at the meeting place, the Nagas who were present got up and walked away. I was distressed, not on my own account, but because the Prime Minister of Burma, an honoured guest of ours, had been treated so discourteously.

Shri Basu has talked about the atrocities of the military and Shri Kamath about Cypriots and Kenyans. I do not know what justification they have for using such language. Then Shri Keishing has referred to the burning of villages and the shooting down of people. In military operations things are not done as if we were sitting in a drawing room. And I do not say that everything that was done can be justified completely. Sometimes mistakes are made. One of the most regrettable mistakes, and one which has distressed us exceedingly, has been in connection with the killing of Dr. Haralu. His sons are important officers of ours – assistant political officers – and his daughter is serving with me in the External Affairs Ministry. It came to me as a tremendous shock when I came back and heard about it, and we took immediate action in regard to it. Courts of Inquiry are carrying on investigation. Undoubtedly, we should punish those who are guilty.

I am not saying that wrong things are not being done there by individuals or groups, whether among the civil authorities or the military. But I do wish to remove the impression that our Army or anybody else there is playing fast and loose with lives, and burning villages. The General Officers Commanding and others have been constantly issuing instructions. It is true that many villages have been burnt there, but our information is that by far the greater part of the burning is done by the Naga hostiles. Shri Jaipal Singh talks about more and more regiments or battalions being sent there. But why do we send them? Principally, in order to protect the people who are being attacked. It is easy to attack in such areas. A group of 10, 20, or 30 persons can go about and attack any village. But it is very difficult to send enough people to protect every village. It is for protection that we have been sending troops to the Naga Hills and adjoining areas. I submit that the general conduct of our forces there has been certainly better than in any similar operation that I know. I believe that Shri Keishing is misled by reports he may receive, if I may say so, from Shri Phizo's publicity department. I get them too, and they are the most fantastic tales one can imagine. They have no relation at all to truth. Sometimes they are sent abroad to foreign newspapers, in America and elsewhere.

When talking of the burnings that have taken place, we must remember, first of all, that the Naga hostiles do it deliberately. Any such group cannot subsist for long unless they get help from the villages if not out of loyalty, at least out of fear. With this threat they go about collecting money and food.

In the Tuensang Division there are at least 100 defence societies of local people, Nagas and others, formed for the protection of villages from hostile Nagas. When the hostiles come, these local people fight them. We have given them some arms. To some extent, therefore, it becomes a civil conflict in the Naga Hills between Nagas and Nagas, and our information is that sometimes villages are burnt in this process. The figure given by Shri Keishing may be correct, but I say that most of these villages have been burnt by the Naga hostiles themselves.

There is a second reason for some of the burning that has taken place. After all these people live in huts with thatched roofs. When any kind of firing takes place between our forces and Naga forces, the firing itself sets fire to the villages. As an Hon'ble colleague reminds me one of the weapons the Nagas use are arrows with burning heads, which are particularly dangerous for thatched roofs. I believe that there were cases in the early days when, our Army, suspecting that some villages had been occupied by these hostiles, directly burnt them or the villages were burnt in the firing. But that kind of thing has been completely stopped, in accordance with our instructions.

I do not for a moment say that there have been no mistakes by civilians or the military. But both in our approach to this problem and, to a large extent, in the carrying out of our directions by the Army we have shown remarkable patience in the face of considerable provocation. Any Hon'ble Member can realize that it is very irritating to be sniped at or to be hit by an arrow or bullet suddenly while going along a road. It makes the average soldier and civilian angry. Nevertheless, our instructions are that patience must be exercised because we want to win over these people.

We are utilizing the co-operation of the Nagas in an increasing measure. There are officials who are Nagas. There are Naga people in our Assam Rifles, and some Naga regiments in our Army. Our definite instructions are that they must seek the co-operation of the Nagas in every way, but make it clear to the hostiles that a person who uses his gun against us will be met with a gun. The Army cannot be withdrawn. That would mean abandoning large numbers of people who have relied upon us for protection. We cannot leave them to be liquidated.

An Hon'ble Member referred to the Naga National Council's agreement with Sir Akbar Hydari and Shri Bardoloi. I do not accept his statement that the agreement has not been honoured. That agreement came up before the Constituent Assembly, or rather before the Special Committee of the Constituent Assembly. All the six Schedules attached to the Constitution were largely drawn up with that agreement in view. It may be that the Sixth Schedule as a whole was not an exact reproduction of the agreement. But the whole object was to give autonomy to their areas and to help them to live according to their own ways. If it is felt that the six Schedules do not go far enough, it is open to Parliament to amend them whenever it likes.

As I said, I met Shri Phizo on three occasions and the other Naga leaders, colleagues of Shri Phizo, once or twice. I have discussed this matter with them and pointed out to them that we are always prepared to consider any constructive proposal for amendment to the provision regarding these areas, but it is no good talking to me about independence for that area. I consider it fantastic for that little corner between China and Burma and India to be called an independent State.

It is true that when they later wanted to see me, certain conditions were attached. The first was that I was not prepared to discuss independence. The second was that they must give up violence. This was before these major acts of violence, when there were only petty acts of violence. I am, as a rule, prepared to meet anybody. But I was told that after each interview with me, these people went back and said that they were on the road to independence, because they met the Prime Minister. They go over the heads of the local Government and local officials and generally try to strengthen their position by reference to the interview they had with me. I felt that if they exploited these interviews in this manner, I should not encourage them. Even then I told them I should be glad to meet them provided they made it clear that they did not demand independence.

The Governor of Assam, as you know, is the Government of India's Agent in regard to NEFA and the problems of NEFA. He has often met the Naga leaders including Phizo. The Chief Minister too has met him more than once. This shows there has been every attempt on our part to meet them and win them over from violence. I do not maintain that every step taken by us or by the State Government has been correct. As an Hon'ble Member said some time ago, what is called Assamization has perhaps been injudiciously pursued. But these are relatively minor things in this picture and the whole object was to deal with the Nagas directly and to establish conditions which would lead to their progress without interference.

I have been anxious that more basic schools should be established there by their own people and that there should be good work on Community Projects in that area. Many Naga boys have gone to Sabarmati to spend some years there and they have gone back as basic school teachers. Community Projects are particularly suited to the conditions in the Naga area, and they could work them with a little help from outside.

I have not referred to the military aspect. Our instructions to the military continue to be what I have just stated: that this problem must be treated as humane problem.

Some Hon'ble Members have referred to general amnesty. Certainly there is a proclamation of amnesty. It is not as though the moment there is a proclamation of amnesty, everybody would automatically and spontaneously surrender. Whoever wants to surrender can avail himself of the amnesty, the period of which we have been extending from time to time. We are not out to punish any individual or any group. We want them to settle down, because it is no pleasure for us to see the great majority of the people there leading abnormal lives.

Does any Hon'ble Member expect Government to invite the leaders of the Naga National Council and treat them as the leaders of a different State and have a treaty with them? We are prepared to talk to any of them but not on the basis of independence. With that sole qualification, they are welcome, if they want to come.

There is no question of prestige. The Government of India's prestige question does not arise when we are dealing with our own countrymen. The Government of India is too big for its prestige to suffer in such small ways. But we cannot take a step which will be misunderstood, misinterpreted and criticized by our own colleagues among the Nagas. Surely, the House will not expect us to betray all those Nagas who, in spite of difficulties, have co-operated with our officials and looked to us for help and protection.

An Hon'ble Member said that the Tuensang Division and the Naga Hills District should be made into a separate political entity. I think he added the Tirap frontier tract too. These are political problems which we can very well consider. But we cannot consider them in this particular context because that will require a change in our Constitution. I have no doubt that the House will agree to change it if it is found necessary and provided the right conditions exist. In this matter, naturally, we have to consult the Assam Government. The main thing is the well-being of the people who live there. It does not matter whether you have one unit or two units. The people in those areas should have a feeling that they can lead their own lives and they should be proud of being citizens of India.

Shri Jaipal Singh has talked about dyarchy and about division of authority between the civilians and the military there. I do not know how far the present arrangements there have come in the way of efficient work. It was our desire not to go too far militarily. That is what led us to send our Army in aid of the civil power. It was easy enough to declare martial law and hand over the whole area to the military, but we did not do so because we have always been against treating this as a purely military problem. In effect, perhaps, the civil power functions there in a very narrow way. Naturally, when armed forces function and have to deal with hostile elements, the civil power's activities are rather limited. But what Shri Jaipal Singh said is a matter worthy of consideration and we shall certainly consider it. I gather from my colleague the Home Minister that the chief function of the civil authorities there is really relief and rehabilitation. In fact, even the Army is doing that. The record of the Army and the civil authorities in regard to the building up of villages and giving relief is indeed creditable.

A proposal has been made that a parliamentary commission should be sent there. I must confess I do not quite understand what a parliamentary commission is going to do and where it will go. Wherever, the commission goes, we will have to send a battalion to protect it. But I hope a time will come when Hon'ble Members of Parliament will be able to visit those areas.

ADIVASI VIDYALAYA*

"Thousands of farmers are coming to Delhi to see the Agricultural Fair, but the young Adivasi Farmers from Bombay State who have come to meet me today are being given training in improved methods of agriculture. I am very happy to know that arrangements are made to train them in scientific methods of agriculture. I am also told that this is a unique institution of its kind in our country to impart such a type of training to Adivasi youths. The time has now come to adopt scientific methods in agriculture to increase our food production and to think such a type of training is very necessary for our farmers. I am glad that Bombay State has started this training and particularly for Adivasis. I am sure that these young farmers will study scientific methods and help our country to produce more food."

* Address to the students of Mahatma Gandhi Adivasi Janata Vidyalaya, Kosad Hill, Bombay State on February 7, 1960.

Excerpts from Speeches Delivered on Various Occasions and Press Conferences

THE COMMISSION*

ONE THING more. A good deal has been said about the Government's indifferent treatment of the Scheduled Castes and Scheduled Tribes. I do not think it would be quite correct to say that it is due to a lack of interest. But it is true to say that much that ought to be done has not been done and cannot be done because of lack of resources and other difficulties. We can appoint a commission if you like. It is easy enough to appoint a commission. But, as the House knows, the appointment of a commission is sometimes only a way out of a difficulty, for it makes people think they are doing something when they really are not doing much. We do not deliberately want to delude the public when we know that we do not have the wherewithal to do much good. I may inform the House that, as far as the appointment of the Special Officer for the Scheduled Tribes and Scheduled Castes is concerned, the President has already decided upon this appointment and if it has not been announced yet it will be announced very soon.

THAKKAR BAPA**

On my return, I have had both good news and bad. The first news that I received filled me with sorrow. This was about the death of that grand old man, Thakkar Bapa, than whom no one has been more devoted to the cause of our backward and under-privileged brothers and sisters, especially the tribal folk.

---

* Speech delivered in Parliament, New Delhi, November, 15, 1950.

** Broadcast from All India Radio, Delhi, January 24, 1951.

Another piece of news related to the settlement in Nepal. It is easy to criticize this as it is to criticize any step; but I am convinced that it was a statesman-like act, on the part of all concerned, to come to this agreement. It marks the beginning of a new era in the history of our sister country. There will be many difficulties ahead and a multitude of problems, but if the people of Nepal and their representatives seek the good of their country with a singleness of purpose and co-operate with one another in this great task, I am sure that success will come to them. The immediate task for the proposed interim Government is to take charge of the administration of the country and to establish peace and order. Nepal is independent and we value her independence. But she is also in close touch with India and, therefore, we have especially welcomed the big step towards democracy that is about to be taken.

Perhaps, our biggest problem at present is that of food or rather the scarcity of it. There is naturally much apprehension and some suffering because of this. As you know, we have tried our utmost to secure food from abroad and we hope that our efforts will succeed. Meanwhile, we have to share such food as we have and this involves a tightening of the belt for all of us. Let each person also remember that he should not have more than his share, for this can only result in others having less than their share.

PROJECTS*

There is always a danger – I am myself guilty of it often enough – that by direction and authority we may make a thing rigid, not flexible, making it a part of the official hierarchy. Now, official hierarchies are, I suppose, necessary. But with all the good they do, they have a certain deadening influence on anything that is spontaneous or vital. Community projects will never grow if they are approached in that way. You must always think of the element of spontaneity.

This kind of project will succeed or fail in the measure that you hieve results within stated periods. There is, of course, a certain an ount of vagueness when you approach the people but there must be precision about one thing: about the time in which a thing must be

* Speech at the Community Project Conference, New Delhi, May 7, 1952.

done. That target must be continually before you. And if you do not reach it, well, you fail to that extent.

Really, what we are committed to is not a few community centres but to working for the biggest community of all and that is the community of the people of India, more especially those who are down and out, those who are backward. There are far too many backward people in this country. Besides the Scheduled Castes and the Scheduled Tribes organizations, there is an organization called the Backward Classes League. As a matter of fact, you can safely say that 96 per cent of the people of India are economically very backward. Indeed, apart from a handful of men, most of the people are backward. Anyhow, we have to think more of those who are more backward because we must aim at progressively producing a measure of equality in opportunity and other things. In the modern world today, you cannot go on for long having big gaps between those who are at the top and those who are at the bottom. You cannot make all men equal, of course. But we must at least give them equality of opportunity.

MANIPUR IN PARLIAMENT*

It is a brief, concise statement, with occasional references to foreign policy or to the next session of Parliament. This session, however, is a budget session and, as such, not much legislation can be undertaken, as is pointed out in the President's Address. In any event, it is neither possible nor desirable that the President's Address should contain long lists of the things we wish to do. Therefore, complaints about the summary nature of the Address betray certain misapprehensions about the situation. An Hon'ble Member from Manipur spoke of the tribal people, in particular about the Nagas. I attach the greatest importance to the tribal people of India and I hope that this House will consider the matter more fully at the proper time, not only because of the large number of tribal folk in the country but also because they have a very special culture which should be protected and encouraged to advance along the lines of its own genius. I do not want the tribal culture of India to be overwhelmed or exploited just because the people to whom it belongs happen to be simple folk.

* Speech delivered in the House of Peoples, New Delhi, May 22, 1952.

PRESS CONFERENCES*

"There must be no attempt to uproot the tribal people from their surroundings; they must not be made to grow soft and thus lose some of their fine qualities."

The Nagas are a fine people, and 'I' like and admire them. The Government of India is determined to help the tribal people to grow according to their own genius and tradition; it is not the intention of the Government to impose anything on them.

The tribes of India possess a variety of culture and are in many ways certainly not backward. But they should always think in terms of India. If that fundamental and most essential fact is forgotten, India will be nowhere.

The people of the tribal areas and the hills attract me greatly and deserve our very special care. I am anxious that they should advance, but I am even more anxious that they should not lose their artistry and joy in life and the culture that distinguish them in many ways.

Looking at other areas outside India, where what are called primitive people live, there are two things affecting them very injuriously. One is the introduction of a market economy in the last century or so. The other was gin or some such alcoholic drink which came from Europe. They got accustomed to it as a result. There was another dangerous thing: they lost their customs. They used to make some kind of handicrafts, etc. You get the most horrid importation from Europe – I am talking about the 19th century or early 20th century – which put an end to the arts and crafts and their simple ways of living. They adopted the so-called European civilization, which was most disastrous. Now, to some extent, there is a danger of the so-called Indian civilization having this disastrous effect, if we do not check and apply it in the proper way.

There are many castes and tribes. Everyone of them has the right to become the Prime Minister or the Rashtrapati of the country. You

* Extracts from Various Press Conferences and Speeches, 1958.

too have got the same right. Any competent man from amongst you can become the Prime Minister or Rashtrapati of this country.

There is a big problem before us. The Adivasis of our country should learn, be educated and cultivate their lands and see that our country progresses. We desire that your customs, traditions and religion should not be interfered with. Some people say that they should be changed. But I do not like that. I want that such arrangements should be made that you should decide for yourself how you would like it to be. Your organizations should remain, song and dances should survive and at the same time you have to work for the progress and prosperity of our great country. We will take your advice and co-operation in the administration of the country.

I am not in favour of a large improvement in literary education in India today. We talk of basic education. We generally adopt resolutions about it. The fact is that we have done very little about real basic education in the country. Now education obviously is necessary to everyone. When I say education I do not mean literacy. If we have to progress economically as a country, we must have much wider education.

Wherever you live, you should live in your own way. This is what I want. You have to decide yourselves how you would like to live. Your old customs and habits are good. We desire that they should survive.

I am anxious that the artistic traditions of the tribal people should be preserved. I have learnt with horror of cheap textiles and other totally unnecessary articles being imported into the NEFA and sold at some Marwari shops which have been opened. I think that such shops should not be permitted there and a list of articles to be imported should be carefully made. We must not encourage the tribal people to get into bad artistic habits which normally follow the wake of what is called civilization.

I am getting a little alarmed when I see not only in this country, but in other countries, great countries, how people are anxious and keen to make others according to their own image or likeness, and impose this way of living or that way of living. We are welcome to it. But why impose our way of living on others who have their own way of living? That applies not only internally but internationally too, and in this great field of foreign affairs, there would be much more peace if people did not want to impose their way of living on other people and other countries.

I am not at all sure which way of living is better, ours or theirs. But in some ways I am quite certain their is better. If that is so, then it is absolute presumption for any of us to approach this problem with an air of superiority, to tell them how to behave or what to do and what not to do and try to make them a second-rate copy of ourselves.

It is a great pity that in large parts of India we have drifted away from the aesthetic side of life. We have still a good deal of folk songs and dances when we go to the villages, because our so-called modern city civilization has not affected them so much as it has affected us. We confine our attention to the cinema which is an excellent medium for good things, but unfortunately, as it is, it is not particularly inspiring. When I look at the progress of what is called modern civilization in India, I see many good things. I see also the lack of many good things. Some of the things lacking here, which I find in the tribal folk, are the spirit of song and dance and enjoyment of life. Therefore, if we go there and meet these people, we must learn and imbibe something of that spirit and not go there with long faces and black gowns and try to kill that spirit among these people.

It is not a question of opening so many schools and so many dispensaries and hospitals. Of course, we want schools and hospitals and dispensaries and roads and all that, but...that is rather a dead way of looking at things. What we ought to do is not merely to put up a school building but somehow to develop a sense of oneness with these people, a sense of unity and understanding. That involves a psychological approach.

You may talk here day after day about development programmes in regard to schools and other matters, but you will fail completely if you do not touch the core of the problem. The problem is to understand these people, make them understand us and create a bond of affection and understanding between us. After the achievement of independence, the basic problem of India, taken as a whole, is one of integration and consolidation. Political integration is now complete but that is not enough. We have to do something much more intimate than political integration and that process takes time. It is not a matter of law. It grows. You cannot force it to grow just as you cannot force a plant or a flower to grow. You can only nurture it and produce conditions where it grows. So the greatest problem of India today is psychological integration and consolidation, to build up a unity which will do away with provincialism, communalism and various other 'isms' which disrupt and separate.

If you approach the tribal people with affection, go to them as a liberating force and as a friend so that they may feel you have come not to take away something from them but to give them something, that is the right integration. But if they feel you have come to try to change their methods of living, to take away their land, to push some of your businessmen there who will exploit them, then it is all completely wrong. The less we hear of this type of integration and consolidation of the tribal areas, the better.

We need some health relief work and cottage industries and the like – simple things which fitted in – but one had always to keep in view the fact that we are going there not to interfere with their way of life but to help them to live it ."

Press Conference about the Visit to Bhutan, October 1958

Speaking on his Bhutan visit, Pt. Nehru advised the authorities in Bhutan not to permit too many outsiders – not even Indians – into their country.

He said he had given the advice to enable the people there to preserve their own customs and manners and ways of life.

India's relations with Bhutan were exceedingly friendly. "It is not on their part any reluctance or any apprehension but it is their general desire not to be overwhelmed by outside – a thing which I perfectly and completely understand."

"We do not encourage, similarly, outsiders to go into NEFA,

which is in India. We do not encourage traders going there and exploiting the people and spoiling all their taste by selling cheap articles normally neither tasteful nor good, uprooting their tribal habits without giving them anything new."

Speech in the Gauhati Congress, January, 1958

The Prime Minister criticized outsiders who sold all sorts of fancy and faked goods to the tribal people and polluted their taste. "Government", he said, "has stopped these things in the NEFA area but people in the valley should also co-operate in this."

Debate in Parliament, March, 1963

"It is wrong to say that we went to keep the people of NEFA as museum specimens. That has never been our policy. Our policy has been based on this fact : that with anyone, more especially the tribal people that to win them over, one has to proceed on well-thought-out plans, to affect their minds and emotions. Normally, what has happened everywhere in the world is this : wherever there were, in some sense, less-advanced people – I use the word 'advanced' with some hesitation but I use it in the normal sense – that is, people who were used to somewhat primitive habits of life, wherever they have come in touch with others more advanced, they have often been almost destroyed. That has been the case in the South Sea Islands, and everywhere. Therefore, one has to proceed with great care."

Debate in Parliament, June, 1958

"I am quite sure that we should prevent mill-cloth from going there (tribal areas) as far as we can."

Nehru on officers serving in NEFA : "The man who goes there as an officer must be prepared to share his life with the tribal folk. He must be prepared to enter their huts, talk to them, eat and smoke with them, live their lives and not consider himself superior or apart."

On emotional integration of NEFA : "Integration in a sense is slowly taking place, but pushing in a few or large numbers of outsiders does not help integration."

SCHEDULED TRIBES*

I am not changing the Constitution by an iota: I am merely making it stronger. I am merely giving effect to the real intentions of the framers of the Constitution and to the wording of the Constitution unless, of course, it is interpreted very narrowly. Looking at the narrow issue that came up in Madras, I shall say that this amendment is not intended to be a communal amendment. We must distinguish between the communal approach and the approach of helping our weaker and more backward brothers and sisters. And, although it is my amendment, I don't particularly like the words "backward class of citizens" and I hope the Select Committee will find some better wording. What I mean is this: it is the backward individual citizens that we should help. Why should we brand groups and classes as backward and forward? It is a fact that certain groups or classes are backward but I do not wish to brand them as such or treat them as such.

In this connection, may I say that a group or class which, perhaps, deserves greater sympathy from this House is the tribal folk, whether in the North-East Frontier tract or in Central India or elsewhere. Many of our colleagues in this House represent the Scheduled Castes and not only help us in our work but keep us informed of the needs of the Scheduled Castes. However, we have very few persons in this House to speak for the Scheduled Tribes. Therefore, it should be the special concern and care of this House to look after the interests of the Scheduled Tribes and their advancement in every way and when we add these words to Article 15, we certainly include the Scheduled Tribes.

LADAKH**

As everyone knows, Ladakh is a part of Kashmir. Kashmir was a State under a Maharaja and the defence of Kashmir lay with the Maharaja except that the Government of India, in British times, could be called upon to help when necessity arose. There was no fear in those days of an attack from the side of Tibet or from any other side on Kashmir.

* Reply to debate in Parliament on the reference to a Select Committee of the Bill to amend the Constitution of India, New Delhi, May 18, 1961.

** Statement in reply to debate in Rajya Sabha, August 22, 1962.

The fear of the British in the old Czarist days was that possibly Russia might come down through Kashmir or through Afghanistan into India. There was this fear of Russia in the British mind right through the 19th century. The Maharaja's government did not consider it at all necessary to protect the eastern borders of Kashmir and Ladakh. There was some slight argument about one or two parts. In fact, there were four or five villages in the heart of Tibet, far from the Ladakh border, which were the *Zamindari* of Kashmir, and every second or third year the Kashmir government sent a little mission to these villages to collect the revenue, Rs. 100 or Rs. 200, in order to assert its *Zamindari* right. The process was peaceful. No question arose of having any prospective apparatus on that border in the Maharaja's time.

A month or two after our independence, came the invasion of Kashmir by the tribals and later by the Pakistani troops. During the fighting in 1948, part of Ladakh was occupied by the Pakistani troops. In fact they cut off the main access to Ladakh which is the road from Srinagar to Leh passing the big pass, Zoji-La, and we were compelled to use another, a difficult and round-about route, from Manali in the Kulu valley over very high mountains, to reach Leh. We did reach Leh. It was a remarkable effort of our Army to drive the Pakistanis from Zoji-La. In fact the Army built the road. It describes a sudden rise of about 2,500 to 3,000 feet winding up the mountain, and from the top of the mountain one sees on the one side the wooded valley of Kashmir and on the other bare tree-less rocks of the uplands of little Tibet as Ladakh is called. Our Army took the tanks up there and drove out the Pakistani troops and gradually assured the protection of Leh and eastern Ladakh. A part of western Ladakh remained in the possession of the Pakistani troops. Included in the area occupied by Pakistan in Kashmir is a part of Ladakh about which she wants to talk to China. This is the background. Just about the time when we were busy fighting the Pakistanis, the Chinese came to Tibet. A great power was next to us. We saw that situation had changed.

Our judgment of the situation was that the danger lay in the NEFA part and, therefore, from then on we tried to protect the NEFA border. Gradually we have built up outposts there and, more important, administration has gradually spread in NEFA. At the same time we thought of Ladakh too. We thought that Ladakh had to be protected, but it was a very difficult task to reach the places where our posts are now located. It takes about three weeks' or a month's journey by road. We sent some small teams to survey, and they went across Ladakh, and that is the evidence we have that no Chinese were there at that time. We established an air field there because we wanted to cover Ladakh and not leave it unprotected. Our Air Force calls it the highest airfield in the world. It is at an elevation of about 14,000 feet. About six or seven years ago I went to that airfield. Therefore, I told Mr. Chou En-lai that I could speak from my own evidence, apart from others' evidence, that I went to the airfield and his people were not anywhere near the place; that I went a second time and I saw his people on a hill-top nearby, and they had come since. He had no particular answer. The main thing is that quite apart from any claims based on history, the Chinese were not there and they are there now. It was a peaceful frontier, and it is not a peaceful frontier now. I was pointing out how difficult it was for us to organize any defence system in Ladakh. We have gradually done it, but we cannot put forward a defence post unconnected with the rest. It has to be in tiers. The very first thing which was necessary was to build the road to Leh. A good road exists now. Other roads also have been built. But mostly our communications are by air and our Air Force has done a very fine piece of work in supplying our posts by air. Those who are actually at the posts are a fine lot of men and I should like to express our high appreciation of them.

This background may lead the House to understand that before the Chinese came to Tibet, we could not hold them at the frontier. The one border which we protected more or less adequately was the NEFA border. I am quite sure if we had not held them there, they would have walked in. They did walk in more or less on the Ladakh border.

One aspect of this trouble which has the character of an opportunist adventure is the fact of Pakistan and China trying to collaborate together in this matter. It is very surprising that Pakistan, which is the champion standard-bearer against communism and is a member of Central Treaty Organisation (CENTO) and South East Asia Treaty Organization (SEATO) should now try to team up with China, and that China should, to some extent, appreciate this and meet it, in spite of their utterly different policies. Apparently the only policy in common between them is dislike for India.

We have to face this situation, and in facing it we have to remember that it is not merely a frontier incursion or aggression. It is something much deeper. It involves the future relationship of two of the biggest countries of Asia. Continuing hostility between India and China will affect us, affect China and affect Asia and will have other far-reaching effects for generations. It will be a tremendous burden for the countries concerned. When the world is changing very fast, for us to be tied up with a continuing war would be unfortunate. At the same time it is obvious that no country worth its grain, and certainly not India, can submit to bullying tactics and to force being used to take its territory and to show that it can be treated casually by any other country. It is impossible, whatever the consequences might be. We have to face this difficult situation with courage and strength. Strength, of course, depends on what we do on the frontier, but strength ultimately depends upon the unity of effort in the country.

BIRTH OF NAGALAND*

Almost exactly two years ago, I made a statement in the House in regard to Nagaland and in regard to a certain agreement which had been arrived at with the leaders of the Naga Convention. What we are doing today is in continuation of that agreement. The agreement has been acted upon during these two years, to the extent it could be, without having an amendment of the Constitution.

We would have had these Bills earlier but for the fact that the situation in Nagaland has not been normal, as the House knows, and we wanted it to approach normality before we took this step. The Provisional Council of Nagaland which was formed as a result of the agreement has been functioning, on the whole, with success. As they desired that further steps should be taken, we thought that the time had come to implement fully the agreement of two years ago.

In effect this House had accepted the basic point which these Bills raise, that is, the creation of Nagaland with certain powers, apart from the details which are given in the Bills. We have acted upon that acceptance during this period.

* Statement in Lok Sabha while moving Bills for the creation of the State of Nagaland, August 28, 1962.

I am happy to be able to move this amendment because it is in continuation of the policy which we have followed throughout in regard to Nagaland. We have never relied merely on using military forces to deal with the situation there, although, unhappily, we had to use them because of the activities of certain hostile elements. We have always made a political approach in order to make these people our friends and citizens of India

After the transfer of power in 1947, the Naga Hills district and the Tuensang district were incorporated in the North East Frontier Agency, and they were included in the Sixth Schedule of the Constitution.

Later, some people in Nagaland area organized armed resistance, and more, there was succession of murders, forcible exactions, arson etc. With great reluctance we had to take military measures or police measures to deal with the situation. Our military and police forces and the Assam Rifles have had an exceedingly difficult time there, in the sense that they had to be held back so that innocent people might not suffer. Occasionally, some innocent people did suffer. We are sorry for that. We even took step to punish those, namely, our forces, who were guilty, although they might have been innocently guilty. In spite of all this, the kind of propaganda that has been made by Mr. Phizo and some of his lieutenants has been quite extraordinary and quite outrageous in its character. I do wish to pay a tribute to the general behaviour of our Army and the Assam Rifles in these hills in the face of exceedingly difficult circumstances.

The difficulties increased. The terrain was also very difficult. There is a frontier with Burma. The hostile Nagas used to retreat to the other side of the frontier where we could not follow them. They found shelter there and came back when they could. This went on for some time. The people of Nagaland became exceedingly weary of the suffering which they underwent and the exactions which were made from them by the hostile elements, and they gathered together in a big convention. It was in 1957. The first demand they made was that the Naga Hills area and the Tuensang Division should be made into a separate unit under the External Affairs Ministry. We acceded to the demand, so that although in theory and constitutionally these areas were still parts of Assam State, they were made into a separate unit under the External Affairs Ministry, that is, under the Government of India. This has continued since then.

I wish to draw special attention to the fact that this has remained a separate unit, because now that it is proposed to form the State of Nagaland, it is largely renaming the area plus giving some powers. The unit has been separate for several years. It is not being created. It has been separate by the decision of Parliament and it has functioned as such. These Bills intend to rename it – even the naming has been practically been done – and to give it certain effect. The separation from Assam took place in December 1957, and that was accompanied by a general amnesty for the release of convicts and under-trial prisoners responsible for offences against the State.

A second convention of the Naga people was held in May 1958. They went to the extent of appointing a liaison committee to contact and win over the misguided Nagas in support of the convention's policy of securing the maximum autonomy for the areas inhabited by the Nagas in order that they could share the responsibilities of the government of Nagaland. This effort, however, did not meet with success.

A third convention was held in Mekokchung in October, 1958, and this prepared a 16-point memorandum for the consideration of the Government. The main demand was for the constitution of a separate State within the Indian Union to be known as Nagaland. A delegation under the leadership of Dr. Imkongliba Ao, president of the convention, met me two years ago in July 1960. That resulted in the agreement to which I referred at the beginning and the matter being subsequently placed before Parliament. A Council was formed and during the last two years it has been functioning as a preliminary to the change-over, and the Governor, although in law he had authority, has acted in accordance with the wishes of the Council of the Nagas.

The House may remember the tragedy when Dr. Imkongliba Ao was shot down by some of the hostiles. That indicates the kind of people the hostiles are. They shot down a great leader of the Nagas who himself had at one time supported them but had subsequently worked for an agreement and for peace and harmony there.

In the agreement which was arrived at, there was a transitional period, as desired by the Naga leaders themselves, during which an interim body consisting of 45 members chosen from the tribes of

Nagaland and a Council of not more than five members from the Interim Body were to be constituted to assist and advise the Governor in the administration of Nagaland. These interim arrangements were brought into force and have been functioning satisfactorily. Elections to the village, range and tribal councils were held and the administration of Nagaland has increasingly become the responsibility of the representatives of the Naga people themselves.

The State of Nagaland Bill which we are considering has certain special provisions. One is that for the time being the Governor will have special powers in regard to law and order and finance, but as soon as the situation is normal, it will not be so. That can be declared by the President. As for finances, the actual income of Nagaland is very little at present. It could be more. The Government of India has been spending a large sum of money on welfare schemes, and we thought that the Governor should have special powers to see that the finances were not misused. The special clauses have been made by the Naga leaders. As soon as the situation improves, the Ministry which will be in existence in Nagaland will be in charge completely.

The Tuensang Division or District of the State of Nagaland has been treated separately. The Tuensang representatives wanted it to be treated separately and the Naga representatives who had come to the convention agreed to that. This area is somewhat more backward than the other two districts of Nagaland. Therefore it has been decided that this area will have a Regional Council and the Governor will play a little greater part in that area for the first ten years, the period being shortened if necessary.

It is proposed that the Governor of Nagaland will also be the Governor of Assam, or the other way about. The Governor of Assam will be the Governor of Nagaland, but he will be there not as Governor of Assam but as Governor of Nagaland. The High Court of Assam will continue to function for Nagaland.

We do not wish to interfere with Naga tribal customs and tribal ways of justice; therefore, we have left these tribal laws intact. Their tribal councils will deal with them.

By these Bills we take an important step, that is, we add to the number of the autonomous States of the Indian Union. The State, for the time being, will have certain restrictions on its autonomy; otherwise, it will be a full State of the Union. In course of time, as the situation returns to normality, it will have all the other powers of a State of the Indian Union. Considering the background of trouble we have had in the area, it is a happy consummation that we solve this question not purely by military means but by this political and friendly approach.

BORDER AREAS*

Apart from the equipment, all our frontiers were hundreds of miles away from the roads, and the roads were to be laid over the most difficult terrain in the world. We had taken this up in hand. We created the Border Roads Organization. They had made hundreds of miles of roads, but still they are incomplete. They are making more and more of them and the Border Roads Organization has done good work. There have been complaints about it, and suspected persons have been tried; but please remember that the Border Roads Organization was operating not just in one place in the NEFA. Its network spreads from U.P., Himachal Pradesh to Ladakh. There are different units, and from almost all these units we have received reports of good work. The one unit of which we did not have good reports was unfortunately of Bomdi La, the Tuskar unit. We enquired into it. Many of these charges made were found to be exaggerated. Some were found to be correct and we are proceeding against the persons, officers and others, who were involved. But, as a whole, the Organization has done well and made roads all over the Himalayas – right up from the borders of Nepal and U.P. to Ladakh. It is an enormous job and they are doing it pretty well. It is also a tremendously long job with thousands of miles of roads being made. I am just pointing out the circumstances in which we are functioning, and which condition our thinking. Some Hon'ble members may think that we were careless with our defence. Of course, it is always possible that if we had foresight and had known exactly what was going to happen, we might have done something else. But, in the nature of things we could not have done very much more. We could not have produced the roads, unless we had built them. It takes much time to modernize an army and we would have to spend vast sums of money. That was the problem before us.

* Reply to the debate on the International situation, Rajya Sabha, September 3, 1963.

TRIBAL DEVELOPMENT*

I am all in favour of machinery. I like the feel of machinery, the look of it, but more and more, I have felt that from the point of view of balanced development, we have to lay greater stress on many small industries in our villages, make them slightly urbanized, lessen the gap between them and the urban areas and increase the facilities available to the people who live there, instead of concentrating on the towns and cities and drawing out people from the villages, thus creating problems in the cities.

Another point is that we in India live in a very mixed society – mixed in terms of development, in terms of human-beings, in terms of the variety in the country and the people. You will find that many people still live as their forefathers lived a thousand years ago or more. You will also find here people who may be said to live in the middle of the 20th century. So, you see in India a mixture of the 10th, the 15th and the 20th centuries. We have vast areas in India which differ from one another. We have a large number of people whom we call 'tribal' people. Many possibly think that 'tribal people' means some kind of primitive people. Well, some tribes are rather primitive, but others are highly developed. They have a different kind of society; they do not have a market economy and do not possess many things that come with the machine age. If I may say so, in many ways, they are far better as human-beings than non-tribal people like me. Because they have not developed their economy in the conventional way, they are called tribals. They are a democratic people. They are fine men and women, and possess many cultural qualities which we do not possess.

So, we have all these mixtures of human-beings in India, a vast number of them and a growing number of them. How should we deal with them? Broadly, we want them to develop according to their own genius. We do not want to impose things upon them.

On the other hand, unless we have some organized scheme of giving them opportunities to develop, they will not develop. Take education, for instance. That is one of the bases of social welfare. At

* Speech delivered at a Seminar on Social Welfare, New Delhi, Sept. 22, 1963.

present, we have, I believe, about 55 million students in our educational institutions. That is a considerable number and it is growing every year. I think in two or three years' time it will be 65 million – practically 100 per cent children of the school-going age. Although our schools may not be very wonderful to look at, although our teachers may not be perfect, the mere fact that 55 million boys and girls go to school is a tremendous development. It is a revolutionary development, and this fact is changing the whole structure of our society. The children who go to school, specially the girls, influence their parents who may be illiterate, and many of whom live in the villages. Their mothers, grandmothers and earlier to them many generations have never been to school. When the children start going to school, they learn new things and tell their parents about them. They introduce little changes in their homes. There is now a very large number of young women going to our colleges.

So, I should like you to think in terms of providing the basic necessities of life to every body in a country like India. I am ashamed to confess that even today, in spite of every effort, there are areas of India where it is difficult to get good water to drink, and people have to go miles and miles to fetch a pot of water. If I may put it so, I should think the very first thing to do in social welfare is to provide water to drink. There must be enough food, clothing, housing, education and health. If we could provide all these to every inhabitant, it does bring a certain basic standard of living to everybody. Having provided that, we can try to raise this standard.

Every country has its own problems and it is rather difficult to generalize, but, in regard to India, I do feel that we should concentrate on giving the mass of people a share in the progress that India is making. We have put up very fine plants, huge plants, hydro-electric schemes and all that, and they are bearing fruit. Yet there are areas in India where no great changes or improvements have come at all. Gradually, no doubt, these improvements will seep down to them. These areas require help.

ILLUSTRATIONS

Jawaharlal Nehru and Indira Gandhi with Tribal Folk Dancers

The Tribals garlanding Panditji

Accepting a *trishul* from a tribal folk-dancer

With the tribals of Madhya Pradesh

With the tribals of Himachal Pradesh

In Gujjar's costume

With Pangwals

Among Gaddis of Himachal Pradesh

With Gujjars of Kashmir

Among the tribals of Madhya Pradesh

With Kerala Folk-dancers

With the tribal dancers of Madhya Pradesh

Two Bastar tribal girls standing with Panditji

In Talkatora Garden

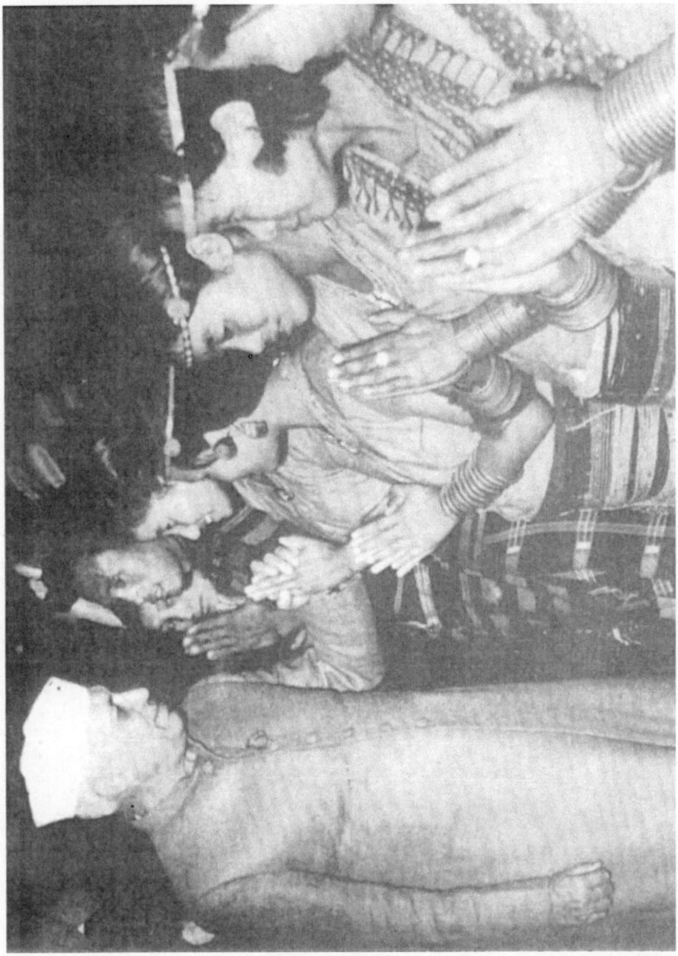

Meeting with Manipuri tribal girls

Sitting dressed in tribal costume with the tribals

Watching two little dancers from Tripura

With Manipuri dancers

Among Todas of Nilgiri

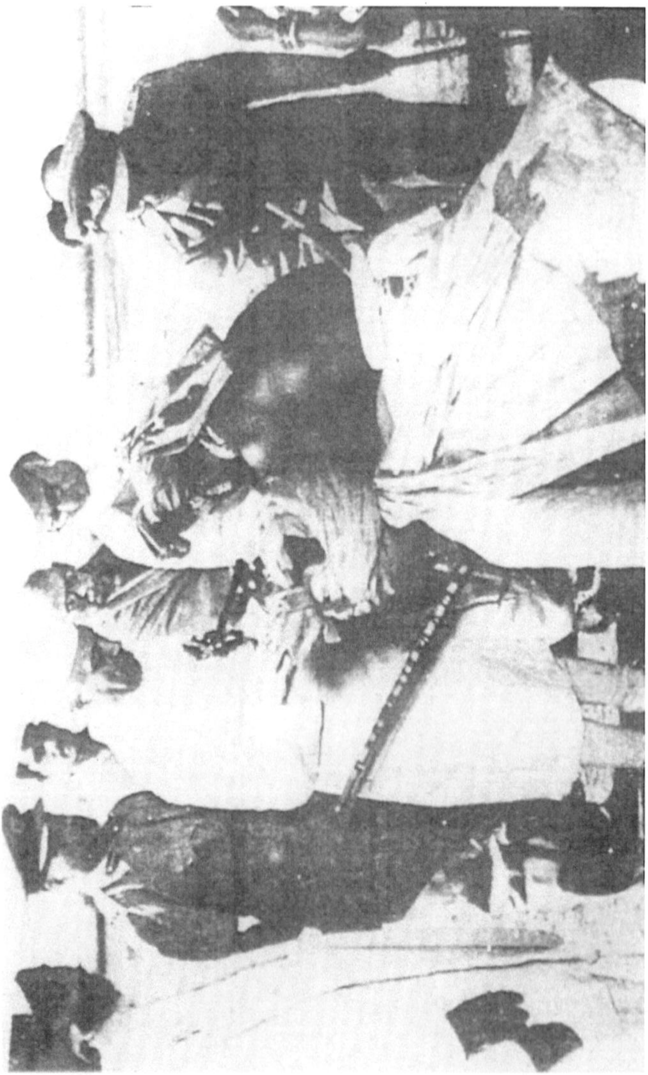

Receiving Presents from a Tribal of Jagdalpur

Tribal dancers with Indira Gandhi and Panditji

Bibliography

Agrawal, S.P. and Aggarwal, J.C., 1989,
Nehru on social issue,
Concept Publishing Company, New Delhi.

Bose, N.K., 1969,
Statement of tribal situation in India,
Indian Institute of Advanced Study, Shimla.

Chatopadhyaya, Kamladevi,
Tribalism in India,
Vikas Publishing House, New Delhi.

Damodaran, A.K., 1988,
Nehru's ideas on social development,
Mainstream 27(7) 12 November p35-38.

Dube, S.C., 1976,
Nehru and tribal India,
Secular Democracy 9(21-22) November p183-84.

Dube, S.C., ed., 1977,
Tribal heritage of India,
Vikas Publishing House, New Delhi.

Haimendortt, C.V.F., 1982,
Tribes in India, struggle for survival,
Oxford University Press, Delhi.

How should we look at the tribal people, 1976,
Yojana (Special Number) 20(13-14) 15 August, p80.

Janardhan Rao, B. and Narendra Babu, P., 1988,
Nehru and policy of tribal integration,
Mainstream 27(7) 12 November, p54-56.

Jayaswal, Sitaram, comp, 1965,
Nehru on society, education and culture,
Vinod Pustak Mandir, Agra.

Joshi, Shashi, 1985,
Nehru on nationalism and socialism,
Mainstream, 24(11-12) 16 November, p14-16.

Kidwai, Anser, 1982,
Nehru's new deal for scheduled tribes,
National Herald (Sunday Herald) 14 November, p11 : 1-6.

Majumdar, D.N. 1950,
Affairs of tribe : A study in tribal dynamics,
Universal Publishers, Lucknow.

Misra, P.K. and Malhotra, K.C., 1962,
Nomads in India,
Anthropological Survey of india, Calcutta.

Nehru, Jawaharlal,
India's independence and social revolution,
Vikas Pub., New Delhi.

Nehru, Jawaharlal, 1946-1964,
Jawaharlal Nehru's speeches, Delhi,
Publications Division, Vol I 1946-49;
Vol II 1949-53: Vol III 1953-57;
Vol IV 1957-63; Vol V 1963-64.

Nehru, Jawaharlal,1964,
A selection from the writings and speeches of Jawaharlal Nehru, 1964,
Seminar 59 July, p9-50.

Roy Burman, B.K., 1972,
Selected Works of Jawaharlal Nehru,
Orient Longman, New Delhi.

Roy Burman, B.K., 1972,
The tribes : The modern phonex (Lectures),
Indian Institute of Advanced Study, Shimla.

Shah, M., ed., 1983,
India : Degradation and development,
Hyderabad Book Trust Publication, Hyderabad.

Shashi, S.S., 1977,
Himachal : Nature's Peaceful Paradise, New Delhi.

Shashi, S.S, 1977,
- A sociological study of Gaddi tribe in Himachal Pradesh, Sterling, New Delhi.

Shashi, S.S., 1977,
Tribal women of India,
Sandeep Prakashan, New Delhi.

Shashi, S.S., 1978,
Shepherds of India,
Sandeep Prakashan, New Delhi.
Shashi, S.S., 1979,
The Nomads of the Himalayas,
Sandeep Prakashan, New Delhi.
Singh, Bhupinder and Bhandari, J.S., 1980,
The tribal world and its transformation,
Concept Publishing Company, New Delhi.
Srivastava, B.N., 1964,
How Nehru saw the tribals,
Vanyajati 12(3) July, p122-25.
Thankappan Nair, P., 1965,
Nehru's philosophy for the tribal people of India,
Modern Review, 117(5) May, p383-89.
Tribe (Udaipur), 1968, 5(2)
Tribe (Udaipur), 1969, 6(1)
Venkata Rao, V., 1987,
Socialist thought of Jawaharlal Nehru,
Indian Journal of Political Science 48(2),
April-June, p195-211.
Vanyajati, (New Delhi), 1953, 3(2) April.
—, —, 1955, 3(1) January.
—, —, 1961, 9(2) April.
—, —, 1962, 10(1) January.
—, —, 1964, 12(3) July.
—, —, 1966, 14 (4) October.
—, —, 1974, 22(4) October.
Vidyarthi, L.P., 1966,
Nehru's approach to tribal culture,
Vanyajati 14(4) October 1966, p170-75.
—, —, 1981,
Tribal development and its administration,
Concept Publishing Company, New Delhi.

Index